CW00418381

CHINESE
ZODIAC
SIGNS

Yi Wah

PUBLISHED BY:
STONE Copyright © 2019

CHINESE ASTROLOGY

The zodiacs originated as a result of Imperial Leader,

who needed to choose twelve animals as palace guards.

The zodiac signs play an important part in the culture of the Chinese as they can be used to determine one's fortune for the year, marriage compatibility, career choices and the best time to have babies.

In some places, married men were accompanied to go out at night with their wives, when it was their zodiac year.

Furthermore, their years were initially known as earthly branches. The branches were also assigned to the hours of the day based on the time of the sun. The Zodiac in

Chinese is important because it represents culture significance in that the animal signs were used in stories too. Apart from showing the years, the Chinese zodiac also had some important features in relation to their culture.

Being that the zodiac recurs after every twelve years, everyone meets his or her birth sign year after a period of twelve years. One's Zodiac sign might be the same as that of any of the family members especially if one is twelve years older or younger than them.

Chinese zodiac was used to tell time. In the early times,

people did not have clocks or watches. They used the twelve earthly branches to name the hours. The Chinese society used the twelve animals to tell time. This also acted as a source of entertainment and convenience to the society. The twelve signs of the Chinese zodiac are believed to be a recurring cycle. The zodiac signs form a recurring twelve-year cycle and each cycle is represented by one of the twelve animals. They believed that the year that one was born determines your zodiac sign. Each zodiac sign represented two hours.

The zodiac year does not start on the beginning of January, rather the New Year's Day falls between mid-January and late February. People feared bad luck because it can bring calamities to them and their families. This is what prompted the society to wear red undergarments and items in order to protect themselves from evil spirits.

Furthermore, each zodiac sign was believed to have a predetermined personality trait in people's lives. The year that a person was born was believed to relate with their zodiac sign. This was also assumed to affect their personality. Their personality was determined by one's birth hour and birth month.

These zodiac signs were also believed to be suitable for choosing the best spouse ad determining the right time to have babies. It was used to determine if two people were compatible with marriage or relationship.

Chinese astrology helps the Chinese culture in providing a detailed understanding of their birth years and the animals that they are related with. This gives the society a deeper understanding.

The Chinese zodiac was most famous for the naming of the years. This was done with the aid of the twelve animals. The twelve animals were believed to have originated when the ruler Ruler wanted palace guards and decided to choose the twelve animals.

DOG

In mythology, a tale states that the Imperial Leader decided the order of animals corresponding to what order they arrived at a gathering he had organized.

Dog arrived eleventh as he was abroad with Rooster and Monkey.

The years corresponding to Dog are Nineteen Thirty-Four, (1934), Nineteen Forty-Six (1946), Nineteen Fifty-Eight (1958), Nineteen Seventy (1970), Nineteen Eighty-

Two (1982), Nineteen Ninety-Four (1994), Two Thousand and Six (2006) and Two thousand and Eighteen (2018).
Dog is loyal, to their careers, loved ones, and friends.

Dogs tend to be very popular, however inside they can feel quite insecure.
Those Men are honest and sincere. They are very family oriented.
Women are more concerned and find it hard to trust. They love being in nature.

Those most compatible with Dog are Tigers, Horse, and Rabbit.

RAT

According to the tales of ancient times, the placing of the animals on the zodiac wheel was determined by their arrival at the gathering organized by the Imperial Leader. After taking a ride on the Ox, the Rat jumped off and ran inside, thus being the very first animal.

Those born in the Year of the Rat are those born in Nineteen Twenty-Four (1924), Nineteen Thirty-Six (1936), Nineteen Forty Eight (1948), Nineteen Sixty (1960), Nineteen Seventy-Two (1972), Nineteen Eighty-Four (1984), Nineteen Ninety Six (1996), Two thousand and eight (2008).

Those born in the Year of the Rat are positive thinkers with lots of energy. Although they mean well, their words can be harsh. They love money and tend to hold on to it tightly.

Those male members are creative yet often lack the determination to follow through on their dreams.

Those female born these years are caring and loving home life.

The signs most compatible with the Rat are the Dragon, the Monkey and the Ox, and most especially the latter.

The colors green blue and gold are Rats luckiest colors.

They have very creative imaginations which make Rats beautiful for any career involved in the arts.

DRAGON

According to ancient legend, the determining of where each animal was to be placed on the zodiac wheel was ordered by their arrival at a gathering the Imperial Leader was holding.

The Dragon arrived fifth and is thus the fifth animal on the zodiac wheel.

Of all the animals, Dragons are by far the most respected animals. Their independence and strength never stop their seeking for love.

Those born in the Year of the Dragon are nineteen Twenty-Eight (1928), Nineteen Forty (1940), Nineteen Fifty-Two (1952), Nineteen Sixty-Four (1964), Nineteen Seventy-Six(1976), Nineteen Eighty-Eight (1988), Two Thousand (2000), Twenty Twelve (2012)

Men born in the year of the Dragon seek a romance

that supports their careers, they care not for wealth, yet do seek fame.

Women Dragons are mighty and captivating and can win most challenges. They demand respect. Like male dragons, their career is important to them.

Dragon is most compatible with the Monkey, the Rooster, and the Rat

Silver, gold, and grey are the luckiest colors for Dragon

OX

Ancient lore speaks of a gathering of animals, held by the Imperial Leader. The place on the zodiac wheel would be decided by the arrival of which the animals arrived to the palace.

Had the Ox not been tricked by the Rat, who jumped

ahead of him, then Ox would have been the very first animal, yet as it stands, he was second.

These wonderful animals, are appreciated immensely, for their hard-work and loyalty.

Those born in the Year of the Ox are Nineteen Twenty-Five (1925), Nineteen Thirty-Seven(1937), Nineteen Forty-Nine (1949), Nineteen Sixty-One (1961), Nineteen Seventy-Three(1973), Nineteen Eighty-Five (1985), Nineteen Ninety-Seven (1997), Two Thousand and Nine (2009), and twenty twenty-one (2021).

The Oxen are natural leaders, hard-working and determined. Their tempers very seldom flair, and they seek no reward, usually very kind and logical.

Male Oxen are honest and loyal, putting all of themselves in with a full heart of devotion. They can be quite demanding of others.

Those female Oxen, are gentle and demure, quick thinkers and somewhat stubborn.

The signs most compatible with the Ox, are the Snake, the Rat and the Rooster.

Green, blue and yellow are the luckiest colours for the Ox.

Their lives are most enhanced by a stable career. Their health is usually very good.

MONKEY

The Monkey is the ninth sign of all zodiac animals in Chinese Astrology. According to a myth, the Imperial Leader said the order of the zodiac animal would be decided by the order in which each animal arrived at his party. As it occurred, the animals arrived at the same time, so the Imperial Leader decided to go by the order that they met the god in the other country.

Monkey became ninth.

The monkey is associated with the Earthly Branch and also the hours 3-5 in the afternoon. It is yang in terms yin and yang. According to Chinese culture, peaches are symbols of longevity and because monkeys like eating them, they are associated with long life. Monkey are seen as animals which can achieve all their dreams because of their lighthearted prankster nature. The most recent Monkey years are 1932, 1944, 1956, 1968, 1980, 1992, 2004, and 2016. There is a 60-year calendric cycle paired with the Celestial Stems, and they cycle through all the five natural elements.

Characteristics and Personality

The most defining trait of a monkey is intelligence. They win accolades and teacher's praises as children and an adult, they make great leaders and are professionally recognized. This led them to be very arrogant. They are most of the time disrespectful and egocentric when making decisions. When others do better than them, monkeys easily become jealous, thus they are not the best when it come to competition, a trait that is both positive and negative. Nevertheless, they see everyone as teachers. Monkeys react very well to critiques and they easily learn from their mistakes. They are composed and logical thinkers. They are always competitive and able to triumph and be the winner at the end.

Characteristics and traits of people born in Monkey Year

Men

They are very enthusiastic and responsible. They have a great sense of humor and can make anyone laugh. They know how to get what they want and they will do it easily.

They are, though, usually stubborn and have some element of immaturity in them. Nevertheless, they are very tolerant. These men unlike other zodiacs, look past most faults in other people. They easily forgive and on many occasions they don't even recall what happened. These men are very problematic too. They find it hard to persevere since their interests are always changing. They are unable to maintain long-term relationships because they are opportunists.

Women

Women born in the monkey year are very social and easily connect with others. Because of their beauty and warm personality, people are normally drawn to them unconsciously.

They maintain very high standards and expectations and are full of ideas and highly competitive. They don't go down easily when faced with hardships. They usually don't need sympathy and comfort from others. They on the hand show overly optimistic because of their confidence. Even so, they are very responsible and flexible. They make new friends easily and adapt quickly to changing environments.

Animals that are most compatible with Monkey are Snake, Rat, and Dragon.

Monkeys have an extreme relationship with snakes. It is either they are the most compatible or clash with the strongest. Although they have similar personalities, one is yin and the other is yang.

Rats, on the other hand, are able to cheer Monkeys up when they are feeling down and it is always full of laughter when they are together.

Dragons can sometimes also bring joy to Monkeys and they are attracted to them too as a strong competitor.

Least compatible animals with Monkeys are Tiger and Pig.

Monkey clash with Tigers strongly as they are suspicious of each other thus fight constantly.

Health

Monkeys believe that being sick is a waste of a valuable day and so they rarely feel ill. They usually remain in good health due to their constant active lifestyles and when they do fall sick, it is because of the nervous feeling.

Career

Monkeys can do just about any kind of work. They are very good at adapting to a changing environment and above all, are very intelligent. Monkeys will often charge double for their services though they will work very quickly. The best career field for them is accounting and banking, engineering, science, traders in the stock market, air traffic control, dealer, film director, jeweler, and sales representative.

Relationships

Monkeys are known to be adamant to settle down because of their general promiscuous nature; which can be attributed to the fact that they are easily bored.

But when they pair up with a perfect match, they usually tend to end this kind of behavior.

Monkeys and the 5 elements

Metal Monkey – Years 1920 and 1980

Metal monkeys are known for being determined and very ambitious as a result, they are often successful. They prefer to be alone despite the fact that they are considered warm-hearted and likable. They are however very loyal to their partners and employers.

Water Monkey – Years 1932 and 1992

They are overly sensitive and often get hurt by things said to them by others. They don't show their sensitive side to the public and as a result, are extreme jokesters. They can succeed about on anything if they stay focused but they most often get easily distracted from their goals.

Wood Monkey – Years 1944 and 2004

The wood Monkeys have exceptional communication

skills which enable them to interact well with the others. They are known to be hard workers who have a profound understanding of the way things function.

Fire Monkey – Years 1956 and 2016

They are full of determination and are excellent at setting and meeting their goals. Their company is enjoyed by others even though these Monkeys always want the upper hand in every situation.

Earth Monkey – Years 1908 and 1968

They are the activists of the community and have an inherent desire to have a normal life. They can be depended on and are serious about their work and relationships. They do everything with 100% efforts and determination and in return they expect others to give them respect.

HORSE

The horse occupies the seventh spot in the rank of zodiac animals. A particular myth postulates that Imperial Leader had set a requirement for in which the position would be determined. It was based on the order in which each of the animals would land to his celebration. Unfortunately, the horse had to bypass a cemetery but was quite petrified. As a result, he took much time running across this path with closed eyes. After walking over this stumbling block, he accelerated and reached the seventh. Besides, it is linked to the Earthly Branch as well as the 11-13 hours at the middle of the day. It also plays a significant role in war and transportation, heading the six domestic animals. What is more, the horse is a symbol of speed and freedom, with some northern communities, for instance,

Mongolians venerating and worshipping it. However, they are often perceived as free spirits, exclusively requiring space to show their true self. The years recently associated with it include

- 1942-
- 1954
- 1966
- 1978
- 1990
- 2002
- 2014
- 2026

The Personality and Character Traits

Indisputably, horses are quite energetic. Both erudite and athletic, they believe in following their dreams to success. Contrary to the expectations, they are motivated by happiness and not riches and fame. They expect the rest to operate as fast as they cannot contextualize the reason for the impossibility. Besides, the contradicting characteristics are attributed to the fact that they often vary emotions. Notably, they are short-tempered and get easily provoked. Nevertheless, once the issue is resolved, they forget faster. One of the most significant challenges they face in the inability to acknowledge their own mistakes.

Men whose birth corresponds with the horse year tend to be independent and yearn for freedom. Most of them are easygoing and dearly handles everyone. They owe their popularity in nearly all groups to their humor and selflessness. They go beyond their capacities in attempts to be helpful to others. While this is a sign of maturity, these individuals mature relatively slower compared to others. One of their significant weaknesses lies with the tendency to overestimate themselves. They find it challenging to make favorable adjustments even if they know their faults in advance.

Similarly, women with birthdays corresponding to the horse year are stunning and give off a refreshing sensation. More often they vary their behavior and attitudes. For instance, at times they may portray themselves as gentle ponies while in other times as wild stallions. Nonetheless, they are outstanding and the best in whatever they do. Furthermore, their success does not depend on motivation or other people's assistance. Unfortunately, they are often characterized by indecisiveness and lack of a clear plan, mostly leaving things to be dictated by fate.

Perfect Careers for Horses

Horses perfectly fit not only technical but also useful work, including journalism and sales among others. Incontrovertibly, such tasks call for reflexes and improvisation. Generally, horses cherish relentlessly changing responsibilities. The reason behind this is just as outlined at the onset; they often change assertiveness and feelings to various things. Moreover, they effectively become accustomed to the ever-changing environments. More often they have definite plans even as others contemplate on various things, a personality that makes them perfect candidates as legislators and decriers. It is prudent to offer horses the freedom they cherish. This will be possible where an individual acknowledges that horses dislike monotonous tasks.

Health and Way of Life

Horses are always in constant motion with regards to goals and targets. Once one is attained, they set another one with no thoughts of resting. The often distraction on their biological clock is attributed to their personality. It is prudent to acknowledge that this condition may result in liver and kidney disorders. Important still, it should be remembered that cold may cause chest pains. However, the conditions mentioned above can be controlled, for instance, by decelerating their fast-paced rhythm.

Generally, Horses enjoy good health naturally. Nonetheless, just as too much of something can be detrimental, it can turn out to be worrisome if they continuously ignore rest. Pulling all-nighters has been a routine for them, and they often work even during on holidays. It is vital that they establish and stick to a controllable lifestyle. Otherwise, it may be a daunting task for them to uphold their health.

SNAKE

The origin of the Chinese Zodiac can be traced back to the period of the Imperial Leader, according to the tales that history presents. Different stories have been told concerning the origin of this Zodiac over the years.

This has made it difficult to decide on the true story to explain their origin. Even so, Chinese culture has incorporated the Zodiac and their beliefs about specific signs have acted as a tool or rather a guideline that shapes the life of the individuals. For instance, the snake Zodiac sign is a representation of a group of people born between specific years.

The Snake Chinese Zodiac sign is perceived to possess specific characteristics that are brought about in the people born in the jurisdiction of this time. For instance, the snake is portrayed as discerning in the manner in which it tactically hid on the hoof of the horse and managed to cross the river, in one of the many tales. With regard to this, people born within the zodiac snake are expected to be intellects. This group of individuals not only display their intelligence in their academics or social interactions, but they also have a sixth sense that enlightens them with effective solutions or rather strategies.

These individuals are also considered thoughtful and are bestowed with wisdom and a deep-thinking understanding of the ideas and the fluctuations of life. Snakes are referred to as the guardians of the treasure. This is for a fact that those born in this zodiac period need a life which is financially stable. The ancient people referred to the snake as the Little Dragon and the skin that it shed was known as the dragon skin. In the Chinese Lunar calendar, it is stated that the snake wakes up from its long hibernation and slithers out of its den on the third day of the third month.

Furthermore, another personality trait of the people born during the snake zodiac sign is that they are restrained, responsive, attractive and full of empathy. In the snake household, quality is embraced as compared to quantity. Elegance and style are also important as it provides deep comfort and luxury, and the reason for this being that these individuals have the desire to achieve. Members of this sign crave peace and tranquility just as the world of the thrust and cut is definitely not meant for the snake. Their mental energy is more important as opposed to their physical dynamism because it is the psychological energy that drives the snake on. These individuals like sitting in a quiet environment just as the snake does not like to be rattled.

When it comes to love life of these individuals, they take their time and are extremely selective people with unmeasurable high standards. Choosing a partner is done with care and discernment. However, once they have committed to someone, they tend to become possessive and jealous. This can be related to the snake in that it can make a powerful friend but a potential enemy. If anyone crosses its path, it will simply take its time until it can strike the most effectively with a deadly aim and no mercy. Snakes are intense lovers and get satisfaction in the pleasures of the flesh.

The snake's beauty, unfathomable intelligence, and sensuality intrigues. They are analytic, , giving them confidence in their day to day lives. Those born in this period experience more opportunities related to business, public relations, and even politics. They are generous beings provided that they get served first. The best jobs and careers for people born during this period are philosophers, librarians, politicians, lawyers, physicians, writers, and even military careers. Their lucky colors are believed to be green and red according to the ancient tales.

In conclusion, the snake Zodiac sign is a representation of a group of people born between specific years. For example, in Chinese culture, the people born between the years, 1905-1917, 194-1953 and 1989-2001. The Chinese zodiac sign snake is believed to possess a variety of qualities such as determination, soft-spoken, sympathetic, passionate and smart. These individuals do not like getting betrayed, and in their love life, once committed to someone else, they become possessive and jealous. They also have the desire to achieve and are always determined in whatever they want to do.

TIGER

Tigers are known for their courage and strength, and *joi de vivre*. As with all Chinese Zodiac signs, the order they come in the Zodiac, according to ancient tales, is the order they arrived in at the gathering held by the Imperial Leader. After somewhat of a scuffle, the Tiger was third.

The years of those born in the year of the Tiger are

Nineteen-Fifty(1950), Nineteen-Sixty-two(1962), Nineteen Seventy-Four(1974), Nineteen-Eighty Six(1986), Nineteen Ninety-Eight(1998), Twenty-Ten(2010), and Twenty-Twenty-Two(2022).

There is no doubt that Tigers are very kind souls, stimulated by innocence and music. Those male born Tigers seek adventure, and love a sense of risk. They can be forceful when they need something to be understood, especially in the work place. Those female born Tigers are completely captivating, and make loving nurturing mothers. They are intelligent and free.

The signs most compatible with Tiger are the Horse, the Dog and also the Pig. Of all of these, mostly the Pig, as they are both wishing to put in the necessary to make the relationship work. However, the sensitive side of the Tiger would only ever be revealed to the loyal Dog.

Tigers portray natural leadership skills. They need much rest for optimum health.

ROOSTER

Ancient lore speaks of the tales of a gathering held by the Imperial Leader. Each zodiac animal arrived at a different time, and the order they arrived determined their place on the zodiac wheel. The Rooster, being in another country, arrived tenth.

Roosters appear sturdy and strong, however this covers a deep vulnerability, and in truth, they need much validation from those they care for most.

The years for those born the year of the Rooster are Nineteen Forty-Five (1945), Nineteen Fifty.Seven(1957), Nineteen Sixty-Nine (1969), Nineteen Eighty-One (1981), Nineteen Ninety-Three (1993), Twenty-Five (2005), and Twenty Seventeen (2017).

Roosters are known for having somewhat of a perfectionist nature, and they will be openly critical of what they believe to be below their high standards.

Female roosters are down to earth, and create harmonious homes as they are highly organised.

Male roosters are wavering in their fluctuating emotions, happy and sad and they are natural problem solvers.

The most compatible sign for the Rooster is the Dragon, due to the Rooster´s admiration of the Dragon. Then the Ox and the Snake are most compatible.

Roosters lucky colours are yellow and gold and brown.

In their professional life, Roosters need a lot of freedom. They make gains and losses easily, receiving financial windfalls, and spending it just as fast. Roosters find family life to be a nurturing and safe haven.

GOAT

In mythology, a tale states that the Imperial Leader decided the order of animals corresponding to what order they arrived at a gathering he had organized.

Goat arrived eighth as he was stranded with Deer.

The years corresponding to Dog are Nineteen Forty-Three, (1943), Nineteen Fifty-five (1955), Nineteen Sixty-Seven (1967), Nineteen Seventy -Nine (1979), Nineteen Ninety-One (1991), Two Thousand and Six (2006) and Two thousand and Three (2003), Twenty Fifteen (2015) and Twenty Twenty-Seven (2027).

One trademark of the goat is their perseverance and determination to overcome any obstacle. Incredibly gentle, they are also strong.

Deliberating extensively is their general mood.

At home in nature, they adore children and tend to be generous in most ways.

Men are helpful and sociable they behave in very gentlemanly ways, always offering assistance when needed.

The female Goat is caring and focused, very detail oriented, with high standards and very organized.

The signs most compatible with the Goat are the Pig and the Rabbit and Horse.

As they are such caring individuals any career in the caring profession or serving others would fit them well. Their sensitivity also makes them good candidates for the arts.

RABBIT

In mythology, a tale states that the Imperial Leader decided the order of animals corresponding to what order they arrived at a gathering he had organized.

Rabbit arrived fourth as he was napping.
The years corresponding to Rabbit are Nineteen Twenty-Seven (1927), Nineteen Thirty-Nine (19439), Nineteen Fifty-One (1951), Nineteen Sixty-Three (1963), Nineteen Seventy-Five (1975), Nineteen Eighty-Seven (1987), Nineteen Ninety Nine (1999) Two Thousand and Eleven (2011).

So soft and sweet is Rabbit! Rabbit is not weak, though others may be fooled. They are strong and confident, yet also quiet.

Rabbit is in constant pursuit of some goal or another. They are attentive and logical, and this leads them steadily toward their goals.

They feel socially vulnerable, and this sometimes causes them to run away and hide.

Men are peace-makers and very well-mannered. The women are social and considerate and fair.

The Goat and the Dog and Pig are the most compatible signs.

Creative careers suit Rabbit well, due to their sensitive nature.

PIG

Why the Pig?

The pig or Boar is a sensualist, faithful both in friendship and relationship, stylish, perfectionist, and hardworking. Also, he is very tolerant and is recognized by others for his kindness and generosity. He is known for his passion, caring and seductive nature. He attracts faithful friends and others seeking to enjoy his benevolent, with his big heart.

The pig, despite his appearance, lacks self-confidence and that is the reason he most often needs a demonstration of love and affection from other people. Additionally, that is another reason he cares so much for his image. Another big trait of his is his love for fashion, and it is one of his favorite topics of discussion whenever he is with friends. The pig cannot bear to be ignored, and one of the things that can give him paralyzing anxiety is the worry for money.

Chinese Pig Horoscope

The Earth Pig is the animal sign for Chinese New Year

2019, which have great benefits to the natives of the previous Chinese zodiac sign of the animal wheel of the lunar calendar.

According to the horoscope, everything that the Pig want to accomplish during the year 2019 will be successful. The greatest source of self-esteem for the Pig is luck and success.

The Pig makes other people envious by his cunningness. This aspect makes new friends come naturally and in huge number, whom they are attracted by his beneficent and luck of aura. These friends normally come with good intentions and bring a natural mutual benefit to their presence. Others though only seek to enjoy shamelessly enjoy the generous and joyful company of the Pig.

Lucky colors of the Year of the Pig 2019

To bring the right balance of energy flow of the year of the Pig, the most favored colors are red and white. It is used in every event, be it fashion trends, weddings, gifts or decorations of homes. Generally, the color red signifies luck, festive seasons, and marriage according to the Chinese tradition. On the other hand, the color white or also off-white, gray, silver and gold is synonymous with the Metal element.

Practices like wearing red and white colored outfits, with jewelry, can help significantly to harmonize the year 2019's energies. It is not necessary that you overdo the white and red colors. All it takes is a little touch of red and white in your daily life. Something worth noting is that having a red wallet or purse will get your fingers to burn by the money it contains.

If you are born during the year of the pig, you are invited to wear bracelets, a red one for that matter, for the entire year. This is meant to stimulate luck in their ife path. The same applies to other 12 Chinese signs when their astrological sign is the current animal year.

Pig Year 2019-

Love Marriage and Birth

Many great things are awaiting the pig in the year 2019. Most importantly love is the most beautiful prospect that awaits the pig in the year 2019. The dating environment is very conducting for the pig, but this could pose a huge problem to the Pig as He is already in a relationship though this will present a perfect opportunity for the Pig to test His charms and passion. On the flip side, this would threaten His marriage and will lead to an escalation of tension, a situation that can be permanent.

However, it's not the Pig who should dial down his desires, rather it is up to his partner who is supposed to tolerate these impulses through the partner can also decide whether he/she has a problem with it or not. The partner can also choose to change him/herself to try and win back his/her beloved back.

There will be numerous social activities during the year 2019. Friendship is easier to form due to the open-mindedness and warm atmosphere during the Pig Year. However, for the single people, or those starting new relationships should be careful not to be so attached to their lover until they start to witness the reciprocity of his/her feelings.

Compatibility between Two Pigs

Two pigs are ideally part of the same love and friendship compatibility triangle. They form a successful functional couple when they are together. However, this is not always unnecessary for couples who belong to the same Chinese zodiac sign.

Money and Career for the Pig In 2019

The year 2019 is the year that will be successful for the pig regarding personal finances according to the Chinese horoscope 2019. The unsuccessful investments form year will start to reap fruits, making the year 2019 a year of the Pigs natives rich. Of course, this is only reassured to the most patient Pig who made a lot of sacrifices along the way and keep on believing that their dreams will come to pass.

Full Pig's Chinese Horoscope

Each month horoscope from 7th December 2018 to 6th

January 2019 for the Chinese zodiac signs which lies in

the period of the Wood Rat Month of 2018 and 2019.

This period is characterized by the dynamic and warm

seasonal cycles during which the family bonds are

highly consolidated, coupled with a surge in the desire

for material possession.

Printed in Great Britain
by Amazon

76169046R00033